# THE BEGINNER'S GUIDE TO PRAYER

# NAMAAZ & DU'AAS

By Prof. Naeem Tariq

AL QALAM ACADEMY

Islamic Centre, Bedford Road, Shelton, Stoke-on-Trent, (UK) ST1 4PL
01782 761533 , 07877 328391 , 07939 736382
Email: ntariqharooni@hotmail.com

- Writer:

  Prof. Naeem Tariq

  (MA Islamic Studies, Pakistan)

- Illustration and design:

  Mujahid Chowhan

- 12th Edition - 2015 - (10,000)

# CONTENTS

21.1.19

# IMAAN MUJMAL (Imaan in brief) اِيمان مُجمَل

| | |
|---|---|
| AAMANTU BILLAHI KAMAA HUWA | اٰمَنتُ بِا للّٰہِ کَمَا ھُوَ |
| BI ASMAAIHEE WA SIFATIHEE | بِاَ سْمَآئِہٖ وَصِفَاتِہٖ |
| WA QABILTU JAMEEA AHKAAMIHEE | وَقَبِلْتُ جَمِیعَ اَحْکَامِہٖ |
| IQRAARUM BILLISAANI | اِقْرَارٌ بِاللِّسَانِ |
| WA TASDEEQUM BIL QALB | وَتَصْدِیقٌ بِالْقَلْبِ |

**Translation:**
*I believe in Allah as He is with all His names and attributes and I have accepted all His commands declaring by the tongue and testifying with the heart.*

# IMAAN MUFASSAL (Imaan in Detail) اِيمان مُفَصَّل

| | |
|---|---|
| AAMANTU BILLAAHI WA MALAAIKATIHEE | اٰمَنْتُ بِاللّٰہِ وَمَلٰٓئِکَتِہٖ |
| WA KUTUBIHEE WA RUSULIHEE | وَ کُتُبِہٖ وَ رُسُلِہٖ |
| WAL YAUMIL AAKHIR | وَالْیَوْمِ الْاٰخِرِ |
| WAL QADRI KHAIRIHEE WA SHARRIHEE | وَالْقَدْرِ خَیْرِہٖ وَشَرِّہٖ |
| MINALLAAHI TA'AALAA | مِنَ اللّٰہِ تَعَالٰی |
| WAL BA'THI BA'DAL MAUT | وَالْبَعْثِ بَعْدَالْمَوْتِ |

**Translation:**
*I believe in Allah and His angels and His books and His Messengers and in the last day and in fate that good and bad is from Allah and the life after death.*

## SEVEN BELIEFS

1. Belief in Allah
2. Belief in Angels
3. Belief in His Books
4. Belief in His Messengers
5. Belief in the Last Day (Day of Judgment)
6. Belief in Fate (that good and bad is from Allah)
7. Belief in the life after Death

## TAWHEED

Oneness of

Allah ta'aala

## RISAALAH

Holy prophet

Muhammad ﷺ is the last

and final Messenger

of Allah ta'aala.

# 1st DECLARATION OF PURITY

## 1st KALIMAH TAYYIB

**LAA ILAAHA ILLALLAAHU** لَآ اِلٰهَ اِلَّا اللّٰهُ

MUHAMMAD-UR-RASOOLULLAH مُحَمَّدٌ رَّسُوْلُ اللّٰهِ

**Translation:**
*There is no god but Allah, Muhammad ﷺ is the Messenger of Allah.*

# 2nd DECLARATION OF EVIDENCE

## 2nd KALIMAH SHEHADAT

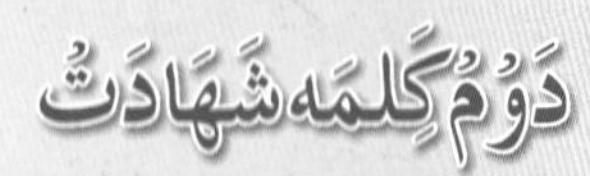


**ASH-HADU ALLAA ILAAHA ILLALLAAHU** اَشْهَدُ اَنْ لَّآ اِلٰهَ اِلَّا اللّٰهُ

WAHDAHU LAASHAREEKA LAHU وَحْدَهٗ لَا شَرِيْكَ لَهٗ

**WA ASH-HADU ANNA MUHAMMADAN** وَ اَشْهَدُ اَنَّ مُحَمَّدًا

ABDUHU WA RASOOLUHU عَبْدُهٗ وَ رَسُوْلُهٗ

**Translation :**
*I testify that there is none worthy of worship except Allah. He is only one. There is no partner for Him. And I testify that Muhammad ﷺ is His Servant and His Messenger.*

# 3rd DECLARATION OF MAJESTY

## 3rd KALIMAH TAMJEED

سومؐ کلمہ تمجید

**SUBHAAN- ALLAAHI WAL- HAMDULILLAAHI** سُبۡحَانَ اللّٰهِ وَالۡحَمۡدُ لِلّٰهِ

**WA LAA ILAAHA ILLALLAAHU WALLAAHU AKBAR** وَلَآ اِلٰهَ اِلَّا اللّٰهُ وَاللّٰهُ اَکۡبَرُ

**WALAA HOWLA WALAA QUWWATA ILLAA** وَلَا حَوۡلَ وَلَا قُوَّةَ اِلَّا

**BILLAAH-HILALIYYIL- AZEEM** بِاللّٰهِ الۡعَلِیِّ الۡعَظِیۡمِ

**Translation**

*Glory be to Allah,and all praise be to Allah and there is no god but Allah and Allah is the greatest and there is no power and might except from Allah, the most High, the most Great.*

# 4th DECLARATION OF ONENESS

## 4th KALIMAH TAOHEED

چہارم کلمہ توحید

**LAA ILAAHA ILLALLAAHU WAHDAHU LAA SHAREEKA** لَآ اِلٰهَ اِلَّا اللّٰهُ وَحۡدَهٗ لَا شَرِیۡکَ

**LAHU LAHUL-MULKU WALAHUL-HAMDU YUHYEE** لَهٗ لَهُ الۡمُلۡکُ وَ لَهُ الۡحَمۡدُ یُحۡیِیۡ

**WA YUMEETU WAHUWA HAYYUL LAA YAMOOTU ABADAN** وَیُمِیۡتُ وَهُوَ حَیٌّ لَّا یَمُوۡتُ اَبَدًا

**ABADAA-ZUL-JALAALI WAL IKRAAMI BIYADIHIL-KHAIR** اَبَدًا ط ذُو الۡجَلَالِ وَالۡاِکۡرَامِ بِیَدِهِ الۡخَیۡرُ

**WA HUWA ALAA KULLI SHAYIN QADEER.** وَهُوَ عَلٰی کُلِّ شَیۡءٍ قَدِیۡرٌ

**Translation:**

*There is none worthy of worship except Allah, He is one, there is no partner for Him. For Him is the kingdom and for Him is all praise. He gives life and causes death. And He is Alive. He will never, ever die, possessor of majesty and reverence. In His hand is goodness. And He has power over everything.*

# 5th DECLARATION OF SEEKING FORGIVENESS

## 5th KALIMAH ISTIGHFAR

## پَنْجُمْ کَلِمَہ اِسْتِغْفَار

| | | |
|---|---|---|
| I seek forgiveness of Allah, my Lord | ASTAGHFIR-ULLAAHA RABBI | اَسْتَغْفِرُاللّٰهَ رَبِّىْ |
| From every sin, | MIN KULLI ZANMBIN | مِنْ كُلِّ ذَنْبٍ |
| I have committed, knowingly or unknowingly, | ADH NABTUHU AMADAN AOW KHATA-AN | اَذْنَبْتُهٗ عَمَدًا اَوْ خَطَاً |
| hiddenly or openly, | SIRRAN AOW ALAANIYATAN | سِرًّا اَوْ عَلَانِيَةً |
| And I make repentance to Him | WA ATOOBU ILAIHI | وَّ اَتُوْبُ اِلَيْهِ |
| from the sins that I know | MINADH-ANMB-ILLADHEE A'LAMU | مِنَ الذَّنْبِ الَّذِىْ اَعْلَمُ |
| and from the sins that I do not know. | WA MINADH-DHANMB-ILLADHEE LAA A'LAMU | وَمِنَ الذَّنْبِ الَّذِىْ لَآ اَعْلَمُ |
| Surely You are the Knower of secrets, | INNAKA ANTA ALLAAMUL GHUYOOBI | اِنَّكَ اَنْتَ عَلَّامُ الْغُيُوْبِ |
| and Concealer of the mistakes | WA SATTAAR-UL-UYOOBI | وَسَتَّارُ الْعُيُوْبِ |
| and Forgiver of the sins | WA GHAFFAAR-UDH-DHUNOOBI | وَغَفَّارُ الذُّنُوْبِ |
| and there is no power and strength | WALAA HOWLA WALAA QUWWATA | وَلَاحَوْلَ وَلَاقُوَّةَ |
| except from Allah, the most High the Greatest. | ILLAA BILLAAHIL ALLIYYIL AZEEM. | اِلَّا بِاللّٰهِ الْعَلِىِّ الْعَظِيْمِ |

# 6th DECLARATION OF DENYING THE KUFR

## 6th KALIMAH RADD-E-KUFR

|  |  |  |
|---|---|---|
| O Allah ! Surely I seek protection with you | ALLAAHUMMA INNEE A'UUDHU BIKA | اَللّٰهُمَّ اِنِّیۡۤ اَعُوۡذُبِکَ |
| from that I associate any thing as partner with You and | MIN AN USHRIKA BIKA SHAI-ANWWA | مِنۡ اَنۡ اُشۡرِکَ بِکَ شَیۡأًوَّ |
| I know it and I seek forgiveness from You | ANAA A'LAMU BIHEE WA ASTAGHFIRUKA | اَنَا اَعۡلَمُ بِهٖ وَ اَسۡتَغۡفِرُکَ |
| for that I do not know it. I repented from it | LIMAA LAA A'LAMU BIHEE TUBTU ANHU | لِمَا لَاۤ اَعۡلَمُ بِهٖ تُبۡتُ عَنۡهُ |
| and I made myself free from disbelief | WA TABARRA' TU MINAL-KUFRI | وَتَبَرَّاۡتُ مِنَ الۡکُفۡرِ |
| and polytheism and the falsehood and the back-biting | WASH-SHIRKI WAL-KIZBI WAL-GHEEBATI | وَالشِّرۡکِ وَالۡکِذۡبِ وَالۡغِیۡبَةِ |
| and the innovation and the tell-tales | WAL-BID'ATI WAN-NAMEEMATI | وَالۡبِدۡعَةِ وَالنَّمِیۡمَةِ |
| and the bad deeds and the blame | WAL-FAWAHISHI WAL-BUHTAANI | وَالۡفَوَاحِشِ وَالۡبُهۡتَانِ |
| and all kinds of Disobedience | WAL-MA'AASII KULLIHAA | وَ الۡمَعَاصِیۡ کُلِّهَا |
| and I submit and I declare that | WA ASLAMTU WA AQOOLU | وَاَسۡلَمۡتُ وَاَقُوۡلُ |
| there is no god but Allah | LAA ILAAHA ILLALLAAHU | لَاۤ اِلٰهَ اِلَّا اللّٰهُ |
| Muhammad ﷺ is the Messenger of Allah. | MUHAMMAD-UR-RASOOLULLAAH. | مُحَمَّدٌ رَّسُوۡلُ اللّٰهِ |

# WUDU (The Ablution)

وُضُو

Wudu is essential before the performace of Salah (Namaz) the process of making Wudu is as following:

1. Firstly ,make Niyyah (Intention) to perform Wudu for the Salah (Prayer) by saying "Bismillah-ir-Rahman -ir-Raheem" بِسْمِ اللّٰهِ الرَّحْمٰنِ الرَّحِيْمِ

2. Then wash both hands up to the wrists three times, making sure that every part including between the fingers is wet by water.

3. Place handful of water into the mouth with the right hand and rinse the mouth three times as shown.

4. Now, put water into the nostrils three times with the right hand and clean the nose with the left hand.

5. Then wash the face three times from hairline of the forehead to below the chin and from one earlobe to the other.

6(a). Thereafter wash the right arm and then the left arm including the elbows, three times.

6(b). Then make khilal of the fingers of both of the hands to make sure that the places in between the fingers are wet.

7(a). Now wet the hands, hold the index finger with the thumb and wipe the head with the remaining of the fingers of both hands from forehead to the back, and then wipe the sides of the
head with the palms of both of the hands passing them from back to the forehead.

7(b). Now rub the front portion of index fingers into the ears and pass the wet thumbs behind the ears.

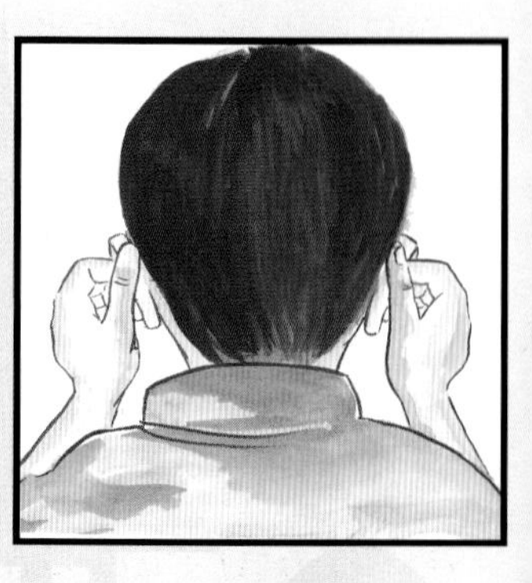

7(c). And then pass the back side of the wet hands over the nape.

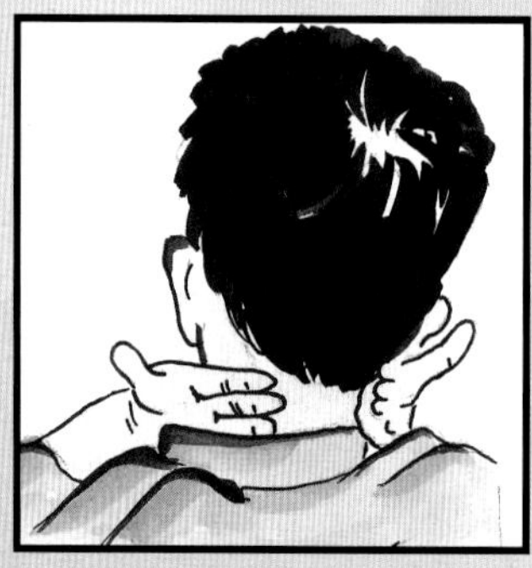

8. Lastly, wash both feet including the ankles starting from the right
foot making sure that the places in between the toes are wet.

# ADHAAN (The call to Prayer)

أَذَان

**Adhaan is an announcement for congregational Prayer. It is Sunnah to say Adhaan for congregational Prayers. The person who says Adhaan is called "Muadhin".The Adhaan should be said standing up ,facing the Ka'bah and by placing the hands over the ears.**

اَللّٰهُ اَكْبَرُ اَللّٰهُ اَكْبَرُ

**ALLAHU- AKBAR -ALLAHU- AKBAR**
*ALLAH IS THE GREATEST -ALLAH IS THE GREATEST*

اَللّٰهُ اَكْبَرُ اَللّٰهُ اَكْبَرُ

**ALLAHU- AKBAR -ALLAHU- AKBAR**
*ALLAH IS THE GREATEST -ALLAH IS THE GREATEST*

اَشْهَدُ اَنْ لَّآ اِلٰهَ اِلَّا اللّٰهُ

**ASH-HADU ALLAA ILAAHA ILLALLAAH**
*I TESTIFY THAT THERE IS NO GOD BUT ALLAH.*

اَشْهَدُ اَنْ لَّآ اِلٰهَ اِلَّا اللّٰهُ

**ASH-HADU ALLAA ILAAHA ILLALLAAH**
*I TESTIFY THAT THERE IS NO GOD BUT ALLAH.*

اَشْهَدُ اَنَّ مُحَمَّدًا رَّسُوْلُ اللّٰهِ

**ASH-HADU ANNA MUHAMMADAR-RASOOLULLAAH**
*I TESTIFY THAT MUHAMMAD ﷺ IS ALLAH'S MESSENGER.*

اَشْهَدُ اَنَّ مُحَمَّدًا رَّسُوْلُ اللّٰهِ

**ASH-HADU ANNA MUHAMMADAR-RASOOLULLAAH**
*I TESTIFY THAT MUHAMMAD ﷺ IS ALLAH'S MESSENGER.*

حَيَّ عَلَى الصَّلٰوةِ

**HAYYA ALAS-SALAAH**
*COME TO THE PRAYER*

حَيَّ عَلَى الصَّلٰوةِ

**HAYYA ALAS-SALAAH**
*COME TO THE PRAYER*

**HAYYA ALAL FALAAH** — حَيَّ عَلَى الْفَلَاحِ
*Come to the success.*

**HAYYA ALAL FALAAH** — حَيَّ عَلَى الْفَلَاحِ
*Come to the success.*

**ALLAHU AKBAR, ALLAHU AKBAR** — اَللّٰهُ اَكْبَرُ - اَللّٰهُ اَكْبَرُ
*Allah is the greatest -Allah is the greatest*

**LAA ILAAHA ILLALLAAH** — لَآ اِلٰهَ اِلَّا اللّٰه
*There is no god but Allah.*

---

*In the adhaan for Fajr (Morning prayer),the following words are added after* **"HAYYA ALAL FALAAH".**

**ASSALAATU KHAIRUM-MINAN NAWM** — اَلصَّلٰوةُ خَيْرٌ مِّنَ النَّوْمِ
*Salah is better than sleep*

**ASSALAATU KHAIRUM-MINAN NAWM** — اَلصَّلٰوةُ خَيْرٌ مِّنَ النَّوْمِ
*Salah is better than sleep*

## IQAAMAH

*When the congregational prayer is ready a second call (IQAAMAH)is recited. It is similar to adhaan except that the following words are added after* **"HAYYA ALAL FALAAH".**

**QAD QAAMATIS-SALAAH** — قَدْ قَامَتِ الصَّلٰوةُ
*The prayer (JAMAAT) is ready*

**QAD QAAMATIS-SALAAH** — قَدْ قَامَتِ الصَّلٰوةُ
*The prayer (JAMAAT) is ready*

# DU'AA AFTER ADHAAN

## دُعا بعد اَذان

| | |
|---|---|
| ALLAAHUMMA RABBA HAADHIHID-DA'WATI- | اَللّٰهُمَّ رَبَّ هٰذِهِ الدَّعْوَةِ |
| TTAAMMATI WASSALAATIL-QAAIMATI | التَّآمَّةِ وَالصَّلٰوةِ الْقَآئِمَةِ |
| AATI SAYYIDANAA MUHAMMADA-NI-LWASEELATA | اٰتِ سَيِّدَنَا مُحَمَّدَانِ الْوَسِيْلَةَ |
| WAL FADEELATA WAD-DARAJAT-AR-RAFEE'ATA | وَالْفَضِيْلَةَ وَالدَّرَجَةَ الرَّفِيْعَةَ |
| WAB'ATH'HU MAQAAMAM MAHMOODA NILLADHI | وَابْعَثْهُ مَقَامًا مَّحْمُوْدَانِ الَّذِیْ |
| WA'ATTAHOO WARZUQNAA SHAFAA'ATAHOO | وَعَدْتَّهٗ وَارْزُقْنَا شَفَاعَتَهٗ |
| YAUM-AL-QIYAAMATI 'INNAKA | يَوْمَ الْقِيَامَةِ ط اِنَّكَ |
| LAA TUKHLIFUL MEEAAD | لَا تُخْلِفُ الْمِيْعَادَ ط |

**TRANSLATION**

*O Allah !O Lord of this perfect invitation and established prayer! Grant Sayyidina Muhammad ﷺ the mediation and the superiority and the Highest rank and honour Him with rank of Mahmood which You have promised Him. And bestow his intercession upon us on the day of judgement. Surely You never go against the Promise.*

# HOW TO PERFORM SALAH (THE PRAYER)

*Before the performance of salah make sure that your Body, dress and the Place where you are going to Pray, are clean. You must know that the Salah which you are performing its time has started.*
*When you are sure that you have fulfilled all of the conditions for Salah, now stand with humbleness to Almighty Allah. And now make intention (Niyyah) to perform the Prayer.*

*Niyyah (Intention)* نِيَّت

**I have made the intention to perform two/ four rakahs fard/sunnah / nafil of today's fajr / zuhr /asr / magrib / isha, worshipping Allah Ta'aala, and facing towards the holy Ka'bah.**

*Now raise both of your hands to the ears touching the ear lobes with your thumbs and say*

**Allahu Akbar.** اَللّٰهُ اَكْبَرُ
*(Allah is the Greatest.)*

*Girls/Ladies lift their hands up to the shoulders only.*

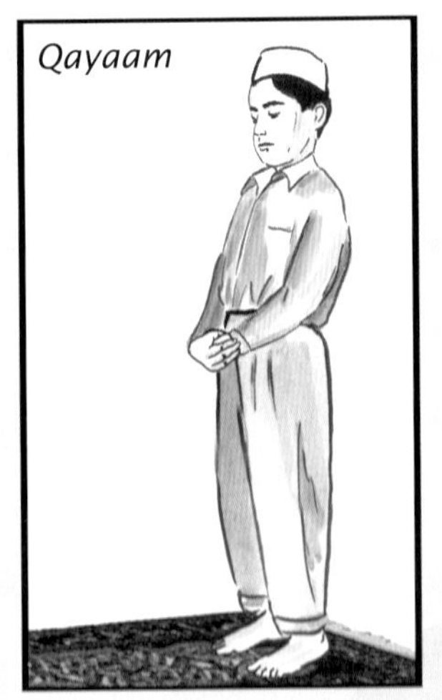


Boys/men Will Keep Feet About Four Fingers Apart, As Shown Above.

*Now placing your right hand on the left, just below or on the navel, and girls/ladies placing their hands on their chest ,recite the following :*

**Thanaa** ——— ثنا

**SUBHAANA KALLAHUMMA WA BI HAMDIKA** سُبحانکَ اللّٰھُمَّ وَبِحَمدِکَ

**WATABAARA KASMUKA WATA AALAA** وَتبارَکَ اسمُکَ وَتعالٰی

**JADDUKA WALAAILAAHA GHAIRUK** جَدُّکَ وَلآ اِلٰہَ غَیرُکَ

**Translation**
*O Allah glory and praise be to You and blessed is Your name and exalted is Your majesty and there is no god but You.*

**Ta'awwudh** ——— تَعوُّذ

**A'OODHU BILLAAHI MINASHAITAANIRRAJEEM** اَعُوذُ بِاللّٰہِ مِنَ الشَّیطٰنِ الرَّجِیم
*I seek refuge in Allah from the rejected satan (devil)*

*Girls/ladies will place hands on chest and keep the feet close to each other as shown.*

**Tasmia** ——— تَسمِیہ

**BISMILLAHIR RAHMAANIR RAHIM** بِسمِ اللّٰہِ الرَّحمٰنِ الرَّحِیم
*In the name of Allah the most kind and merciful*

**Faatihah** ——— فَاتِحہ

**AL'HAMDU LILLAHI RABBIL AALAMEEN** اَلحَمدُ لِلّٰہِ رَبِّ العٰلَمِینَ

**ARRAHMAANIRRA HEEM** اَلرَّحمٰنِ الرَّحِیمِ

**MALIKI YAUMIDDEEN** مٰلِکِ یَومِ الدِّینِ

**IYYAAKA NA' BUDU WAIYYAAKA NASTAEEN** اِیَّاکَ نَعبُدُ وَاِیَّاکَ نَستَعِینُ

**IHDI NASSIRAATAL MUSTAQEEM** اِهدِنَا الصِّرَاطَ المُستَقِیمَ

SIRAATALLADHEENA ANAMTA ALAIHIM صِراطَ الَّذِينَ اَنعمتَ عَلَيهِم

GHAIRIL MAGHDOOBI ALAIHIM غَيرِ المَغضُوبِ عَلَيهِم

WALADHAALLEEN (AAMEEN) وَلاَ الضَّآلِّينَ (اٰمِين)

**Translation**

*All praises be to Allah, Lord of the worlds. The Beneficent, The Merciful. Master of the Judgement day. You alone do we worship and You alone we ask for help. Show us the straight path. The path of those whom You have favoured. Not the path of those who earned Your anger nor the path of those who went astray.*

Surah (Ikhlaas) سُورَةُ (اِخلاص)

QUL HUWALLAHU AHAD قُلْ هُوَ اللّٰهُ اَحَدٌ

ALLAHUSSAMAD اَللّٰهُ الصَّمَدُ

LAM YALID WALAM YOOLAD لَمْ يَلِدْ وَلَمْ يُولَدْ

WALAM YAKULLAHOO KUFUWAN AHAD وَلَمْ يَكُنْ لَهُ كُفُوًا اَحَدٌ

*Translation*

*Say, Allah is one. Allah is Eternal and Absolute. None is born of Him nor was He born. And there is none like Him.*

Allahu Akbar. اَللّٰهُ اَكْبَر

*(Allah is the Greatest.)*

*Now go into the bowing position (Rukoo) place the hands on your knees and recite the following tasbeeh atleast three times.*

SUBHANA RABBI YAL AZEEM سُبحَانَ رَبِّيَ العَظِيم

*Glory be to my Lord, The Most Great.*

*Boys/Men will hold both the knees with the fingers apart, And ensure that the arms do not touch the body.*

*Girls/Ladies should only bend over sufficiently so that hands reach the knees. And the hands should be placed on the knees , with the fingers kept Together.*

*Now come to the standing position and whilst coming up say:*

**SAMI ALLAHU LIMAN HAMIDAH** سَمِعَ اللّٰهُ لِمَنْ حَمِدَهُ

*Allah has heard those who praised Him.*

*(To say these words is called "Tasmee")*
*Then in the standing position say:*

**RABBANAA LA-KAL HAMD.** رَبَّنَا لَكَ الْحَمْدُ

*O our Lord Praise be to You.*

*(To say these words is called "Tahmeed")*
*(To stand up after Rukoo is called "Qawmah".)*
*now saying,*

**"Allahu akbar"** اَللّٰهُ اَكْبَرُ

*kneel down for the prostration with knees touching the ground first then hands then nose and then forehead. And now in the position of Sajdah (Prostration) recite these words three times at least.*

**SUBHANA RABBI YAL A'LAA** سُبْحَانَ رَبِّيَ الاَعْلٰى

*Glory be to my Lord the Most High.*

*(Boys/Men ) the arms should not touch the side of the body nor the ground. stomach should be away from the thighs. And the feet should be up right with the toes pointing toward the Qiblah.*

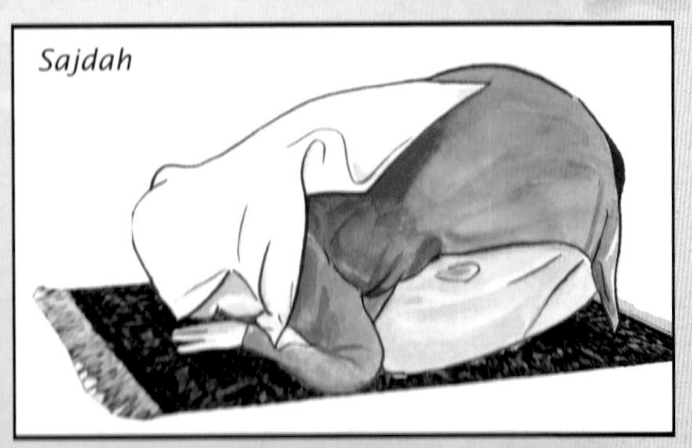


*(Girls/Ladies) in Sajdah: stomach and thighs should be kept together and feet should be spread towards the right side.*

*Now, saying "ALLAHU AKBAR" اَللّٰهُ اَكْبَرُ sit upright with knees still on the ground.*
*To sit between the two Sajdahs is called "Jalsah."*

Jalsah

*Second Sajdah*
*Now, again saying "ALLAHU AKBAR" اَللّٰهُ اَكْبَرُ go into Sajdah position, and perform the second Sajdah same as the first one. In the second Sajdah as before recite the following words three times at least:*

**SUBHANA RABBI YAL A'LAA** سُبْحَانَ رَبِّىَ الْاَعْلٰى
*Glory be to my Lord the most high.*

*This completes one Rakah (unit)of Salah. Now, saying"ALLAHU AKBAR" اَللّٰهُ اَكْبَرُ stand up for the second Rakah, and complete the "second Rakah" in the same way as the first one. The second Rakah is same like the first one except neither thana nor ta'awwudh are read in second Rakah. After completing the second Sajdah of second Rakah saying "ALLAHU AKBAR" اَللّٰهُ اَكْبَرُ sit up in the position of Qa'dah and recite "Tashahhud".*

Jalsah

## Tashahhud تَشَهُّد

**ATTAHIYYAATU LILLAAHI WASSALAWAATU** اَلتَّحِيَّاتُ لِلّٰهِ وَالصَّلَوٰتُ

**WATTAYYIBAATU ASSALAAMU ALAIKA** وَالطَّيِّبَاتُ اَلسَّلَامُ عَلَيْكَ

**AYYUHANNABIYYU WARAHMA TULLAAHI** اَيُّهَا النَّبِىُّ وَرَحْمَةُ اللّٰهِ

**WA BARAKAATU HOO** وَبَرَكَاتُهٗ

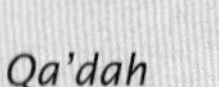

Qa'dah

Qa'dah

Second Sajdah

Second Sajdah

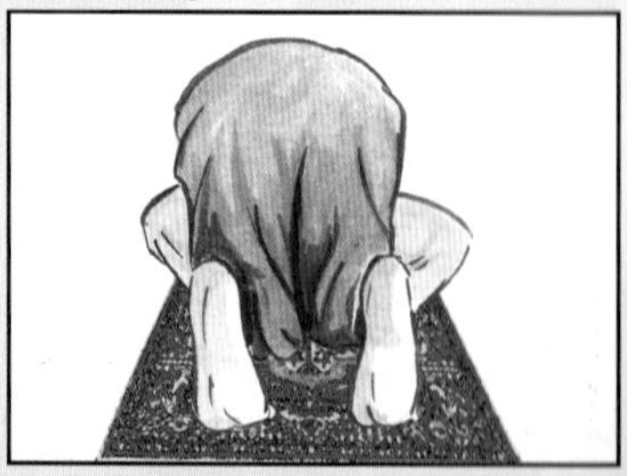

During Tashahhud On the word "Allaailaaha" اَنْ لَّاۤ اِلٰهَ raise the Index Finger as shown and lower it at "Illallaah". اِلَّا اللّٰهُ

ASSALAAMU ALAINAA WA ALAA اَلسَّلَامُ عَلَيْنَا وَعَلٰى

IBAADILLAA HISSAALI HEEN عِبَادِ اللّٰهِ الصّٰلِحِيْنَ

ASH-HADU ALLAA ILAAHA ILLALLAAHU اَشْهَدُ اَنْ لَّاۤ اِلٰهَ اِلَّا اللّٰهُ

WA ASH-HADU ANNA MUHAMMADAN وَاَشْهَدُ اَنَّ مُحَمَّدًا

ABDUHU WA RASOOLUH. عَبْدُهٗ وَرَسُوْلُهٗ

**Translation**

*All the prayers through words, actions and sanctity are for Allah only. Peace be upon you o Prophet, and the mercy of Allah and His blessings. Peace be upon us and all the righteous Servants of Allah. I bear witness that none is worthy of worship except Allah, and I bear witness that Muhammad ﷺ is His Servant and Messenger.*

*At the end of "Tashahhud"stand up for the third Rakah, if you are performing three or four Rakah Salah. Otherwise if it is a two rakah salah, keep sitting and after Tashahhud recite Durood (Blessing on the Holy Prophet), and Du,aa.*

## Durood shareef دُرُوْدُ شَرِيْفُ

ALLAAHUMMA SALLI ALAA MUHAMMADIN اَللّٰهُمَّ صَلِّ عَلٰى مُحَمَّدٍ

WA ALAA AALI MUHAMMADIN KAMAA وَّعَلٰۤى اٰلِ مُحَمَّدٍ كَمَا

SALLAITA ALLA IBRAHEEMA WA-ALAA AALI صَلَّيْتَ عَلٰۤى اِبْرَاهِيْمَ وَعَلٰۤى اٰلِ

IBRAHEEMA INNAKA HAMEEDUM-MAJEED اِبْرَاهِيْمَ اِنَّكَ حَمِيْدٌ مَّجِيْدٌ

**ALLAHUMMA BAARIK ALAA MUHAMMADIN** اَللّٰهُمَّ بَارِكۡ عَلٰى مُحَمَّدٍ

**WA-ALAA AALI MUHAMMADIN** وَّعَلٰٓى اٰلِ مُحَمَّدٍ

**KAMAA BARRAKTA ALAA IBRAHEEMA** كَمَا بَارَكۡتَ عَلٰٓى اِبۡرَاهِيۡمَ

**WA-ALAA AALI IBRAHEEMA** وَعَلٰٓى اٰلِ اِبۡرَاهِيۡمَ

**INNAKA HAMEEDUM MAJEED** اِنَّكَ حَمِيۡدٌ مَّجِيۡدٌ

**Translation**

*O Allah shower Your mercy on Muhammad and His family as you showered Your mercy on Ibraheem and His family. Truly You are the Praise-worthy and Glorious. O Allah shower Your blessings on Muhammad and His family as You showered Your blessings on Ibraheem and His family. Truly You are the Praise-worthy and Glorious.*

## Du'aa دُعَا

**RABBIJ ALNII MUQEEMA-SSALAATI** رَبِّ اجۡعَلۡنِىۡ مُقِيۡمَ الصَّلٰوةِ
*My Lord, make me establisher of Prayer*

**WA MIN DHURRIYYATII RABBANAA WA TAQABAL** وَمِنۡ ذُرِّيَّتِىۡ رَبَّنَا وَتَقَبَّلۡ
*and also my children. Our Lord, and accept*

**DU'AA - RABBANA -GHFIRLEE** دُعَآءِ ۝ رَبَّنَا اغۡفِرۡلِىۡ
*my prayer. Our Lord, forgive me*

**WALIWAALIDAYYA WA LILMUMINEENA** وَلِوَالِدَىَّ وَلِلۡمُؤۡمِنِيۡنَ
*and my parents and the believers*

**YAUMA YAQOOMUL HISAAB.** يَوۡمَ يَقُوۡمُ الۡحِسَابِ
*on the Day of Judgement.*

**Salaam:** *Now, turn your face to the right saying "Salaam" in these Words:*

**ASSALAAMU ALAIKUM WARAHMATULLAAH** اَلسَّلَامُ عَلَيۡكُمۡ وَرَحۡمَةُ اللّٰهِ

*And lastly repeat the same words turning your head to the left.*

*This completes two rakahs of salah.*

*If you are performing a three rakah salah like Maghrib or four rakah of Zuhr 'Asr or Isha salah' then stand up after "Tashahhud" saying "Allaahu-Akbar" and recite "Alfatiha". when you are offering Fard salah do not recite any additional passage or Surah from the Holy Quran after "Alfatiha" in the last two rakahs. After the second Sajdah in the fourth rakah say "Tashahhud", Durood shareef , Dua and end with saying Salaam first to right and then left .*

# NAMES AND TIMINGS OF SALAH

| | | |
|---|---|---|
| 1. Fajr | *(From dawn until just before sunrise)* | صَلَاةُ الْفَجْرِ |
| 2. Zuhr | *(Between midday and afternoon)* | صَلَاةُ الظُّهْرِ |
| 3. Asr | *(From late afternoon until before sunset)* | صَلَاةُ الْعَصْرِ |
| 4. Maghrib | *(From just after sunset until daylight ends)* | صَلَاةُ الْمَغْرِبِ |
| 5. Isha | *(From nightfall until dawn)* | صَلَاةُالْعِشَاء |

*IT IS PROHIBITED TO PRAY AT THE FOLLOWING THREE TIMES.*

1. *At the beginning of sunrise until 15 minutes after full sunrise.*
2. *At mid-day until the Sun begins to decline.*
3. *At the beginning of sunset until it is fully set.*

# TABLE OF THE RAKAHS

| | SUNNAH | FARD | SUNNAH | NAFL | WITR | NAFL | TOTAL RAKAHS |
|---|---|---|---|---|---|---|---|
| FAJR | 2 | 2 | | | | | 4 |
| ZUHR | 4 | 4 | 2 | 2 | | | 12 |
| ASR | 4★ | 4 | | | | | 8 |
| MAGHRIB | | 3 | 2 | 2 | | | 7 |
| ISHA | 4★ | 4 | 2 | 2 | 3 | 2 | 17 |
| JUM'A | 4 | 2 | 4+2 | 2 | | | 14 |

★ *These Sunnah of ASR and ISHA are Ghair Mu'akkida (Occasional)*

*Performance of 4 Fard of ZUHR, ASR, and ISHA.*

| | | | | | | | |
|---|---|---|---|---|---|---|---|
| 1st RAKAH | Thana | Faatihah | Surah | | | | |
| 2nd RAKAH | | Faatihah | Surah | Tashahhud | | | |
| 3rd RAKAH | | Faatihah | | | | | |
| 4th RAKAH | | Faatihah | | Tashahhud | Durood | Du'aa | Salam |

*Performance of 3 Fard of MAGHRIB*

| | | | | | | | |
|---|---|---|---|---|---|---|---|
| 1st RAKAH | Thana | Faatihah | Surah | | | | |
| 2nd RAKAH | | Faatihah | Surah | Tashahhud | | | |
| 3rd RAKAH | | Faatihah | | Tashahhud | Durood | Du'aa | Salam |

*Note: WITR prayer is also performed in the same way but Surah and Qunoot is added in 3rd Rakah*

*Performance of 2 Fard of fajr*

| 1st RAKAH | Thana | Faatihah | Surah | | | | |
|---|---|---|---|---|---|---|---|
| 2nd RAKAH | | Faatihah | Surah | Tashahhud | Durood | Du'aa | Salam |

*Note: 2 Rakah of Sunnah and 2 Nafl are also performed in this manner.*

*Performance of 4 Sunnah Mu'akkadah*

| 1st RAKAH | Thana | Faatihah | Surah | | | | |
|---|---|---|---|---|---|---|---|
| 2nd RAKAH | | Faatihah | Surah | Tashahhud | | | |
| 3rd RAKAH | | Faatihah | Surah | | | | |
| 4th RAKAH | | Faatihah | Surah | Tashahhud | Durood | Du'aa | Salam |

*Performance of 4 Sunnah Ghair Mu'akkadah of ASR and ISHA.*

| 1st RAKAH | Thana | Faatihah | Surah | | | | |
|---|---|---|---|---|---|---|---|
| 2nd RAKAH | | Faatihah | Surah | Tashahhud | Durood | Du'aa | |
| 3rd RAKAH | Thana | Faatihah | Surah | | | | |
| 4th RAKAH | | Faatihah | Surah | Tashahhud | Durood | Du'aa | Salam |

# SOME IMPORTANT DU'AAS AFTER PRAYER

*You can make du'aa in your own words and language after the prayers asking for forgiveness and mercy from Allah Ta'aala but you receive more blessings from Allah Ta'aala if you make du'aa in Arabic.*
*Some of the important du'aas are given below to memorise.*

**1**

|  |  |  |
|---|---|---|
| *O Allah! You are the peace,* | ALLAAHUMMA ANTASSALAAMU | اَللّٰهُمَّ اَنْتَ السَّلَامُ |
| *and peace comes from You, You are Exalted,* | WA MINKA-SSALAAMU TABAARAKTA | وَمِنْكَ السَّلَامُ تَبَارَكْتَ |
| *O Lord of Majesty and Honour.* | YAA DHAL JALAALI WAL IKRAAM | يَا ذَالْجَلَالِ وَالْاِكْرَامِ |

**2**

|  |  |  |
|---|---|---|
| *O our Lord! grant us good in this world,* | RABBANAA AATINAA FI-DDUNYAA HASANATAN | رَبَّنَآ اٰتِنَا فِي الدُّنْيَا حَسَنَةً |
| *and good in the hereafter,* | WA-FIL-AAKHIRATI HASANATAN | وَّفِي الْاٰخِرَةِ حَسَنَةً |
| *and save us from punishment of Hellfire.* | WAQINAA AZAABA-NNAAR | وَّقِنَا عَذَابَ النَّارِ |

**3**

|  |  |  |
|---|---|---|
| *O our Lord! we have wronged ourselves* | RABBANAA ZALAMNAA ANFUSANAA | رَبَّنَا ظَلَمْنَآ اَنْفُسَنَا |
| *And if you do not forgive us and shower mercy upon us* | WA IN-LLAM TAGHFIRLANAA WA TARHAMNAA | وَاِنْ لَّمْ تَغْفِرْلَنَا وَتَرْحَمْنَا |
| *Then surely we will be among the losers.* | LANAKUNANNA MINA-LKHAASIREEN | لَنَكُوْنَنَّ مِنَ الْخٰسِرِيْنَ |

# SALAT-UL-WITR

In Isha prayer the three rakaahs of salaat-ul-witr are wajib (necessary).The first two rakaahs of salaat-ul-witr are performed same as the first two rakaahs of salaat-ul-Maghrib. In the third rakaah after Al-Fatihah, an additional surah or verses of the Holly Quran are to be recited. After which you raise your hands to the ears and say "ALLAHU AKBAR" and fold them again and now recite the following Du'aa. This is called "Dua-al-Qunuut

## DUA-AL-QUNUUT دُعَاءُ الْقُنُوْت

|  |  |  |
|---|---|---|
| O Allah we seek Your help and forgiveness, | ALLAHUMMA INNAA NASTAINUKA WA NASTAGHFIRUKA | اَللّٰهُمَّ اِنَّا نَسْتَعِيْنُکَ وَنَسْتَغْفِرُکَ |
| We believe in You and we rely on You, | WA NU'MINU BIKA WA NATAWAKKALU ALAIKA | وَنُؤْمِنُ بِکَ وَنَتَوَکَّلُ عَلَيْکَ |
| And we praise You in the best way. | WA NUTHNII ALAIKAL KHAIRA | وَنُثْنِيْ عَلَيْکَ الْخَيْرَ ط |
| We thank You and we are not ungrateful to You. | WA NASHKURUKA WALAA NAKFURUKA | وَنَشْکُرُکَ وَلَا نَکْفُرُکَ |
| We cast off and we leave those who disobey You. | WA NAKHLA,U WA NATRUKU MAN-YAFJURUK. | وَنَخْلَعُ وَنَتْرُکُ مَنْ يَّفْجُرُکَ ط |
| O Allah You alone we worship and to You we pray, | ALLAHUMMA IYYAAKA NA'BUDU WALAKA NUSALLII | اَللّٰهُمَّ اِيَّاکَ نَعْبُدُ وَلَکَ نُصَلِّيْ |
| And we prostrate to You and we rush and turn towards You, | WA NASJUDU WA ILAIKA NAS'AA WA NAHFIDU | وَنَسْجُدُ وَاِلَيْکَ نَسْعٰى وَنَحْفِدُ |
| And we hope for Your mercy and we fear Your punishment. | WA NARJU RAHMATAKA WA NAKHSHAA ADHAABAKA | وَنَرْجُوْا رَحْمَتَکَ وَنَخْشٰى عَذَابَکَ |
| Surely Your punishment is close to the unbelievers. | INNA ADHAABAKA BILKUFFAARI MULHIQ. | اِنَّ عَذَابَکَ بِالْکُفَّارِ مُلْحِقٌ ط |

# SALATUT-TARAWEEH

Taraweeh is a special prayer offered in the Holy month of Ramadhan. After isha prayer but before the salaat-ul-witr. Taraweeh may be performed alone but collective prayer is recommended which is usually led by a Hafiz. It has twenty rakaahs and they are offered two by two with a short pause after every four rakaahs. After every four rakaahs the following Tasbeeh should be recited.

(TASBEEH TRAWEEH) تَسْبِيح تراويح

| | | |
|---|---|---|
| All Glory be to the Lord of Power and Kingdom, | SUBHAANA DHIL-MULKI WAL-MALAKOOT. | سُبْحَانَ ذِی الْمُلْكِ وَالْمَلَكُوتِ ط |
| All Glory be to the possessor of the Nobility and the Greatness and the | SUBHAANA DHIL-IZZATI WAL-AZMATI WAL-HAYBATI | سُبْحَانَ ذِی الْعِزَّةِ وَالْعَظَمَةِ وَالْهَيْبَةِ |
| Majesty and the Authority and The Grandeur and the Dominance. | WAL-QUDRATI WAL-KIBRIYAA'I WAL-JABAROOT. | وَالْقُدْرَةِ وَالْكِبْرِيَاءِ وَالْجَبَرُوْتِ ط |
| All Glory be to the King who is Ever-living ,who | SUBHAAN-AL-MALIKIL-HAYYILLA-DHI | سُبْحَانَ الْمَلِكِ الْحَيِّ الَّذِی |
| neither sleeps nor dies. | LAA YANAAMU WALAA YAMUUT. | لَا يَنَامُ وَلَا يَمُوْتُ ط |
| The Glorified, The Holy, our Lord and | SUBBUUHUN QUDDUUSUN RABBUNAA | سُبُّوحٌ قُدُّوسٌ رَبُّنَا |
| Lord of the angels and the soul. | WARABBUL- MALAAIKATI WAR-RUUH. | وَرَبُّ الْمَلٰٓئِكَةِ وَالرُّوْحِ ط |
| O Allah, protect us from the hell fire, | ALLAAHUMMA AJIRNAA MINAN-NAARI | اَللّٰهُمَّ اَجِرْنَا مِنَ النَّارِ |
| O protector, O protector, O Protector. | YAA MUJEERU YAA MUJEERU YAA MUGEER. | يَامُجِيْرُ يَا مُجِيْرُ يَا مُجِيْرُ ط |
| Blessings be upon Muhammad ﷺ | AS-SALAATU BAR MUHAMMAD. | اَلصَّلٰوةُ بَرْ مُحَمَّدٍ ط |

# AYAT-UL- KURSI

There is an extra special verse in the Holy Quran, which is called AYAT-UL-KURSI (Al-Baqara-225).According to the sayings of Holy prophet Muhammed ﷺ this is the greatest verse of the Book of Allah. If you recite "Ayat-ul-kursi" before going to bed, Allah Ta'aala will appoint a guardian upon you all night and the devil will not come near you til morning.

اَللّٰهُ لَآ اِلٰهَ اِلَّا هُوَ ط اَلْحَيُّ الْقَيُّوْمُ ج

ALLAHU LAA ILAAHA ILLAAHUWAL HAYYUL QAYYUUM
Allah! there is no god but Him,the Ever-living,the Sustainer and the Protector.

لَا تَاْخُذُهٗ سِنَةٌ وَّلَا نَوْمٌ ط

LAA TA'KHUDHU-HU SINATUNW-WALAA NAWM
Neither slumber nor sleep overtake Him.

لَهٗ مَا فِي السَّمٰوٰتِ وَمَا فِي الْاَرْضِ ط

LAHU MAA FISSAMAAWAATI WAMAA FIL-ARD.
To Him alone belongs whatever is in the heavens and whatever is in the earth.

مَنْ ذَا الَّذِيْ يَشْفَعُ عِنْدَهٗٓ اِلَّا بِاِذْنِهٖ ط

MAN DHALLA DHII YASHFA'U INDAHOO ILLAA BI'IDHNIHII
Who is there that can intercede with Him except with His permission?

يَعْلَمُ مَا بَيْنَ اَيْدِيْهِمْ وَمَا خَلْفَهُمْ

YA LAMU MAA BAINA AIDEEHIM WAMAA KHALFAHUM,
He knows all that was before them ,and all that shall be after them.

وَلَا يُحِيْطُوْنَ بِشَيْءٍ مِّنْ عِلْمِهٖٓ

WALAA YUHEETUUNA BISHAY'INM-MIN ILMIHEE
And they can grasp nothing of His knowledge

اِلَّا بِمَا شَآءَ

ILLAA BIMMA SHAA'A.
except that which He wills.

وَسِعَ كُرْسِيُّهُ السَّمٰوٰتِ وَالْاَرْضَ ج

WASIA KURSIYYUHUS-SAMAAWATI WAL-ARD.
His Throne extends over the heavens and the earth,

وَلَا يَـُٔوْدُهٗ حِفْظُهُمَا ج

WALAA YAUDUHU HIFZUHUMAA
and preservation of earth and heaven does not weary Him.

وَهُوَ الْعَلِيُّ الْعَظِيْمُ

WA HUWAL ALIYY-UL-AZEEM.
And He alone is the Most High, the Most Great.

# THE FUNERAL PRAYER

"Salat ul Janazah" is a prayer to Allah Ta'aala for a deceased muslim. This salah is offered in congregation but it has neither Ruku nor Sajdah. Four "TAKBEERS" are cecited in it and it is performed standing from the start through to the end. The body of the deceased person is placed infront of the congregation.

Below is the method for performing the Funeral prayer.

INTENTION

First of all make intention saying: "I have made the intention to perform four "TAKBEERS" of the Funeral prayer, Thana for Allah Ta'aala, Darood for the Holy prophet ﷺ and Du'aa for the deceased ,facing the Holy ka'bah, following the Imam.

FIRST TAKBEER

Now following the Imam, raise your hands up to the ears, saying Allahu Akbar اَللّٰهُ اَكْبَر and place them on or below the navel and then recite Thanaa in the following words silently:

|  |  |  |
| --- | --- | --- |
| Glory and praise be to you, O Allah | Subhaanaka-llaahumma wa bi hamdika | سُبْحَانَكَ اللّٰهُمَّ وَ بِحَمْدِكَ |
| Blessed is Your Name and exalted is Your Majesty | Wa tabaaraka-smuka wa ta-aalaa jadduka | وَتَبَارَكَ اسْمُكَ وَتَعَالٰى جَدُّكَ |
| And Glorious is Your praise and there is no god but You. | Wa jalla thanaa 'uka walaa ilaaha ghairuk. | وَجَلَّ ثَنَاءُكَ وَلَآ اِلٰهَ غَيْرُكَ |

SECOND TAKBEER

Then after Thanaa, following the Imam, say Allahu Akbar اَللّٰهُ اَكْبَر silently, without raising your hands to the ears and recite "Durood shareef" silently.

THIRD TAKBEER

After "Durood shareef" following the Imam, say Allahu Akbar اَللّٰهُ اَكْبَر once again, without raising your hands to the ears and then recite one of the following Du'aas accordingly.

# DU'AA-AL-JANAZAH FOR ADULT

|  |  |  |
|---|---|---|
| O Allah forgive our living and our deceased , | Allahumma-ghfir lihayyinaa wamayyitinaa | اَللّٰهُمَّ اغْفِرْ لِحَيِّنَا وَمَيِّتِنَا |
| And our present and the absent and our young | Wa shaahidinaa wa ghaaibinaa wa saghiirinaa | وَشَاهِدِنَا وَغَآئِبِنَا وَصَغِيْرِنَا |
| And our old and our males and females. | Wa kabiirinaa wa dhakarinaa wa unthaanaa | وَكَبِيْرِنَا وَذَكَرِنَا وَاُنْثَانَا ط |
| O Allah whoever You keep alive of us | Allaahumma man ahyaytahuu minnaa | اَللّٰهُمَّ مَنْ اَحْيَيْتَهٗ مِنَّا |
| Keep him alive upon Islam | Fa-ahyihii alal-islami | فَاَحْيِهٖ عَلَى الْاِسْلَامِ |
| And whoever of us you cause to die | Wa man tawaf-faytahuu minnaa | وَمَنْ تَوَفَّيْتَهٗ مِنَّا |
| Let him die in state of iman (Faith) | Fa-tawaffahuu alal-imaan. | فَتَوَفَّهٗ عَلَى الْاِيْمَانِ ط |

# DU'AA-AL-JANAZAH FOR A BOY

|  |  |  |
|---|---|---|
| O Allah make him a source of salvation for us, | Allaahummaj-alhu lanaa faratan- | اَللّٰهُمَّ اجْعَلْهُ لَنَا فَرَطًا |
| And make him means of reward and treasure for us, | Wajalhu lanaa ajran-wa dhukhran- | وَّاجْعَلْهُ لَنَآ اَجْرًا وَّذُخْرًا |
| And make him intercessor for us and one whose intercession is accepted. | Wajalhu lanaa shafianwa mushaffa'aa. | وَّاجْعَلْهُ لَنَا شَافِعًا وَّمُشَفَّعًا ط |

# DU'AA-AL-JANAZAH FOR A GIRL

|  |  |  |
|---|---|---|
| O Allah make her a source of salvation for us, | Allaahummaj-alhaa lanaa faratan- | اَللّٰهُمَّ اجْعَلْهَا لَنَا فَرَطًا |
| And make her means of reward and treasure for us, | Wajalhaa lanaa ajran-wa dhukhran- | وَّاجْعَلْهَا لَنَآ اَجْرًا وَّذُخْرًا |
| And make her intercessor for us and one whose intercession is accepted. | Wajalhaa lanaa shaafiatan-wa-mushaffa'ah. | وَّاجْعَلْهَا لَنَا شَافِعَةً وَّمُشَفَّعَةً ط |

FOURTH TAKBEER

After du'aa following the Imam ,say Allahu Akbar, اَللّٰهُ اَكْبَر again , without raising your hands to the ears.

SALAAM

Finally just after the fourth Takbeer , following the Imam turn your face to the right and say ,

"ASSALAMU ALAYKUM WA RAHMATULLAAH." اَلسَّلَامُ عَلَيْكُمْ وَرَحْمَةُ اللّٰه

And then turn your face to the left repeating the same words silently.
This completes the Funeral prayer.

# The Eid Prayer

Muslims celebrate two Eids every year. Eid-ul-Fitr is celebrated on the 1st of Shawwal, just after the Holy month of Ramadan and Eid-ul-Adhaa is celebrated on 10th of
Dil-Hajj.
The time for both Eid Prayers starts from 20 minutes after sunrise and stays until before noon. Eid Prayer is of two rakaahs. The procedure of the Eid prayer is as follows:

INTENTION

I make intention to perform two Rakaahs of Eid-ul-Fitr\Eid-ul-Adhaa for Allah Ta'aala, with six additional Takbeers, facing the direction of Ka'bah, following the Imam.

In the first Rakaah, after the recitation of Thana, the Imam raises his hands three times to the ears with Takbeer (ALLAHU AKBAR) dropping them each time to the sides and the whole congregation follows. Hands are placed under the navel after the third Takbeer and the Imam recites Al-Fatihah followed by an additional passage and completes the first Rakaah.

In the second Rakaah the remaining three Takbeers are performed after the recitation of Al-Fatihah and an additional passage, just before the Ruku. After that prayer is completed in the usual manner.

"Khutbah"(The sermon) is Sunnah in Eid prayer, which is delivered by the Imam after the prayer.

# MASNUUN DU'AAS

## AT THE TIME OF EATING

BISMILLAAHI WA-ALAA BARAKATI LLAAH

بِسۡمِ اللّٰهِ وَعَلٰى بَرَكَةِ اللّٰهِ

In the name of Allah and with the blessing from Allah.

## IF FORGET TO SAY "BISMILLAH"

BISMILLAAHI AWWALAHU WA AAKHIRAHU

بِسۡمِ اللّٰهِ اَوَّلَهٗ وَ اٰخِرَهٗ

In the name of Allah, the start of it and the end of it.

## DU'AA AFTER FINISHING THE MEAL

ALHAMDU LILLAAHILLADHI AT'AMANAA WA
SAQAANAA WA JA'ALANAA MINAL MUSLIMEEN.

اَلۡحَمۡدُلِلّٰهِ الَّذِیۡ اَطۡعَمَنَا وَ
سَقَانَاوَجَعَلَنَامِنَ الۡمُسۡلِمِیۡنَ

All praise be to Allah who gave us food and drink and made us Muslims.

## WHILE DINING AT THE OTHER'S TABLE

ALLAAHUMMA AT'IM MAN AT'AMA-NII
WASQI MAN SAQAANII.

اَللّٰهُمَّ اَطۡعِمۡ مَّنۡ اَطۡعَمَنِیۡ
وَاسۡقِ مَنۡ سَقَانِیۡ ط

O Allah Feed him who fed me and give him drink who gave me drink.

## WHEN LEAVING THE HOME

بِسْمِ اللّٰهِ تَوَكَّلْتُ عَلَى اللّٰهِ

Bismillaahi tawakkaltu alallaah.

In the name of Allah , I trust upon Allah.

## WHEN ENTERING THE HOME

بِسْمِ اللّٰهِ وَلَجْنَا وَبِسْمِ اللّٰهِ خَرَجْنَا

Bismillaahi walajnaa wa bismillaahi kharajnaa

وَعَلَى اللّٰهِ رَبِّنَا تَوَكَّلْنَا.

Wa alallaahi rabbinaa tawakkalnaa

With the name of Allah we enter, and with the name of Allah we step out and we trust our Lord.

## WHEN ENTERING THE MOSQUE

اَللّٰهُمَّ افْتَحْ لِىْ اَبْوَابَ رَحْمَتِكَ

Allaahumaftah lee abwaaba rahmatik.

O Allah open for me the doors of Your Mercy.

## WHEN LEAVING THE MOSQUE

اَللّٰهُمَّ اِنِّىْ اَسْئَلُكَ مِنْ

Allaahumma innii asaluka min

فَضْلِكَ وَرَحْمَتِكَ

Fadlika wa rahmatik

O Allah I ask You for Your favour and Your Mercy.

## AT THE TIME OF GOING TO BED

بِاسْمِكَ اللّٰهُمَّ اَمُوْتُ وَاَحْىٰ

BI-ISMIKA ALLAAHUMMA AMUTU WA AHYAA.

With Your name ,O Allah, I shall die and I shall live.

# AT THE TIME OF TRAVELLING

سُبْحَانَ الَّذِىْ سَخَّرَلَنَا هٰذَا
وَمَا كُنَّا لَهٗ مُقْرِنِيْنَ ط وَاِنَّآ
اِلٰى رَبِّنَا لَمُنْقَلِبُوْنَ ط

**SUBHANALLADHII SAKH-KHARA LANA HADHAA**
**WAMAA KUNNAA LAHU MUQRINIIN WA INNAA**
**ILAA RABBINAA LA-MUNQALIBOON.**

Pure is He who granted us with the control of this (vehicle),and we were unable to control it. And surly we are to return to our Lord.

# AT THE TIME OF AWAKENING

اَلْحَمْدُلِلّٰهِ الَّذِىْ اَحْيَانَا بَعْدَ
مَا اَمَاتَنَا وَ اِلَيْهِ النُّشُوْرُ

**ALHAMDU LILLAHIL-LADHII AHYAANAA BA'DA**
**MAA AMAATANAA WA ILAYHIN-NUSHOOR.**

All praise be to Allah who gave us life after causing us to die and towards Him is the ultimate return.

# WHEN ENTERING THE TOILET

اَللّٰهُمَّ اِنِّىْ اَعُوْذُبِكَ
مِنَ الْخُبُثِ وَالْخَبَائِثِ ط

**ALLAAHUMMA INNII A'UUDHU BIKA**
**MINAL KHUBUTHI WAL KHABAAITH.**

O Allah, I seek refuge with You from the bad male and female devils.

# WHEN LEAVING THE TOILET

اَلْحَمْدُلِلّٰهِ الَّذِىْ اَذْهَبَ
عَنِّى الْاَذٰى وَعَافَانِىْ ط

**ALHAMDU LILLAAHILLA-DHII ADH-HABA**
**ANNI-L-ADHAA WA AAFAANII.**

All praise be to Allah who removed impurity from me and granted me relief.

## WHILE LOOKING IN THE MIRROR

ALLAAHUMMA ANTA HASSANTA KHALQII — اَللّٰهُمَّ اَنْتَ حَسَّنْتَ خَلْقِىْ

FAHASSIN KHULUQII — فَحَسِّنْ خُلُقِىْ

O Allah, You beautified my body so beautify my manners too.

## WHEN WEARING A NEW DRESS

ALHAMDU LILLAAHILLA-DHII KASAANII — اَلْحَمْدُ لِلّٰهِ الَّذِىْ كَسَانِىْ

MAA UWAARI BIHII AURATII — مَا اُوَارِىْ بِهٖ عَوْرَتِىْ

WA ATAJAMMALU BIHII FII HAYAATII. — وَاَتَجَمَّلُ بِهٖ فِىْ حَيَاتِىْ

All praise be to Allah who granted me dress, that I cover my nakedness with it
and I beautify my life with it.

## DU'AA FOR SEHRI (BEGINNING FAST)

WA BI SAWMI GHADIN NAWAITU MIN SHAHRE RAMADAN — وَبِصَوْمِ غَدٍ نَّوَيْتُ مِنْ شَهْرِ رَمَضَانَ ط

I intend to keep the fast tomorrow in the month of Ramadan.

## DU'AA FOR IFTAAR (BREAKING FAST)

ALLAAHUMMA INNEE LAKA SUMTU WABIKA AAMANTU — اَللّٰهُمَّ اِنِّىْ لَكَ صُمْتُ وَبِكَ اٰمَنْتُ

WA ALAIKA TAWAKKALTU WA ALAA RIZQIKA AFTARTU — وَعَلَيْكَ تَوَكَّلْتُ وَعَلٰى رِزْقِكَ اَفْطَرْتُ

Oh Allah, I have fasted for You, I have believed and relied on You
and I break my fast with the provision from You

# THE LAST TEN SURAHS OF THE HOLY QURAN

## THE MANKIND (SURATUN- NAAS) سُوْرَةُ النَّاس

| | | |
|---|---|---|
| In the name of Allah the Most Kind ,the Most Merciful. | BISMILLAAHIR-RAHMAANIR-RAHEEM | بِسْمِ اللّٰهِ الرَّحْمٰنِ الرَّحِيْمِ |
| Say (O Prophet):I seek refuge in the Lord of mankind. | QUL A'UDHU BIRABBINNAAS. | قُلْ اَعُوْذُ بِرَبِّ النَّاسِ ۙ |
| King of mankind. God Of mankind. | MILIKIN-NAAS. ILAAHIN-NAAS. | مَلِكِ النَّاسِ ۙ اِلٰهِ النَّاسِ ۙ |
| From the evil of the sneaking whisperer, | MIN SHARRIL WASWAASIL KHANNAAS. | مِنْ شَرِّ الْوَسْوَاسِ الْخَنَّاسِ ۙ |
| Who keeps whispering in the hearts of mankind, | ALLADHI YUWASWISU FI SUDOORINNAAS. | الَّذِیْ یُوَسْوِسُ فِیْ صُدُوْرِ النَّاسِ ۙ |
| From among the jinn and mankind. | MINAL JINNATI WANNAAS. | مِنَ الْجِنَّةِ وَالنَّاسِ ۧ |

## THE DAWN (SURATUL FALAQ) سُوْرَةُ الْفَلَق

| | | |
|---|---|---|
| In the name of Allah the Most Kind the Most merciful. | BISMILLAAHIR-RAHMAANIR-RAHEEM | بِسْمِ اللّٰهِ الرَّحْمٰنِ الرَّحِيْمِ |
| Say (O Prophet):I seek refuge in the Lord of the Daybreak, | QUL A'UDHU BIRABBIL FALAQ. | قُلْ اَعُوْذُ بِرَبِّ الْفَلَقِ ۙ |
| From the evil of that which He has created, | MIN SHARRI MA KHALAQ. | مِنْ شَرِّ مَا خَلَقَ ۙ |
| And from the evil of darkness when it is overspread, | WA MIN SHARRI GHAASIQIN IDHA WAQAB. | وَمِنْ شَرِّ غَاسِقٍ اِذَا وَقَبَ ۙ |
| And from the evil of these women who blow upon knots, | WA MIN SHARRIN-NAFFAATHAATI FIL-UQAD. | وَمِنْ شَرِّ النَّفّٰثٰتِ فِی الْعُقَدِ ۙ |
| And from the evil of the envier when he envies. | WA MIN SHARRI HAASIDIN IDHA HASAD. | وَمِنْ شَرِّ حَاسِدٍ اِذَا حَسَدَ ۧ |

## THE SINCERITY (SURATUL IKHLAAS) سُوْرَةُ الْاِخْلَاص

|  |  |  |
|---|---|---|
| In the name of Allah the Most Kind , the Most Merciful. | BISMILLAAHIR-RAHMAANIR-RAHEEM. | بِسْمِ اللّٰهِ الرَّحْمٰنِ الرَّحِيْمِ |
| Say (O Prophet): HE is Allah, the One. | QUL HUWALLAAHU AHAD. | قُلْ هُوَ اللّٰهُ اَحَدٌ ج |
| Allah, the Eternal and the Absolute. | ALLAAHUS-SAMAD. | اَللّٰهُ الصَّمَدُ ج |
| None is born of Him, nor was He born. | LAM YALID WALAM YUULAD. | لَمْ يَلِدْ وَلَمْ يُوْلَدْ لا |
| And there is none equal to Him. | WA LAM YAKUL-LAHUU KUFUWAN AHAD. | وَلَمْ يَكُنْ لَّهٗ كُفُوًا اَحَدٌ ع |

## THE FLAME (SURATUL LAHAB) سُوْرَةُ اللَّهَب

|  |  |  |
|---|---|---|
| In the name of Allah the Most kind, the Most Merciful. | BISMILLAAHIR-RAHMAANIR-RAHEEM. | بِسْمِ اللّٰهِ الرَّحْمٰنِ الرَّحِيْمِ |
| May the both hands of abu Lahab Perish and he will perish. | TABBAT YADAA ABEE LAHABIN-WATABB. | تَبَّتْ يَدَآ اَبِيْ لَهَبٍ وَّتَبَّ ط |
| His wealth and his earnings will not save him. | MAA AGHNAA ANHU MAALUHUU WAMAA KASAB. | مَآ اَغْنٰى عَنْهُ مَالُهٗ وَمَا كَسَبَ ط |
| Soon he will enter a blazing Fire, | SAYASLAA NAARAN DHAATA LAHAB. | سَيَصْلٰى نَارًا ذَاتَ لَهَبٍ صلے ج |
| And his wife too, the carrier of Fuelwoods, | WAMRA-ATUHU HAMMAALATAL-HATAB. | وَّامْرَاَتُهٗ ط حَمَّالَةَ الْحَطَبِ ج |
| Will have a rope of palm upon her neck. | FI JIDIHAA HABLUM-MIMMASAD. | فِيْ جِيْدِهَا حَبْلٌ مِّنْ مَّسَدٍ ع |

## THE HELP (SURATUN NASR) سُوۡرَةُ النَّصۡر

|  |  |  |
|---|---|---|
| In the name of Allah , the Most Kind , the Most Merciful. | BISMILLAAHIR-RAHMAANIR-RAHEEM. | بِسۡمِ اللّٰهِ الرَّحۡمٰنِ الرَّحِيۡمِ |
| When the help of Allah comes and the victory, | IDHAA JAA'A NASRULLAAHI WAL FATH. | اِذَا جَآءَ نَصۡرُ اللّٰهِ وَالۡفَتۡحُ ۙ |
| And you see the people entering | WARA'AITANNAASA YADKHULUUNA | وَرَاَيۡتَ النَّاسَ يَدۡخُلُوۡنَ |
| The fold of the Religion of Allah in troops. | FII DEENILLAAHI AFWAAJAA. | فِىۡ دِيۡنِ اللّٰهِ اَفۡوَاجًا ۙ |
| Then you perform the praise of your Lord and ask His forgiveness. | FASABBIH BIHAMDI RABBIKA WASTAGHFIRH | فَسَبِّحۡ بِحَمۡدِ رَبِّكَ وَاسۡتَغۡفِرۡهُ ؕ |
| Surely He is ever-forgiving. | INNAHUU KAANA TAWWAABAA. | اِنَّهٗ كَانَ تَوَّابًا ࣖ |

## THE DISBELIEVERS (SURATUL KAFIROON) سُوۡرَةُ الۡكٰفِرُوۡن

|  |  |  |
|---|---|---|
| In the name of Allah , the Most Kind, the Most Merciful. | BISMILLAAHIR-RAHMAANIR-RAHEEM. | بِسۡمِ اللّٰهِ الرَّحۡمٰنِ الرَّحِيۡمِ |
| Say (O Prophet):O disbelievers | QUL YAA AYYUHAL KAFIRUUN. | قُلۡ يٰۤاَيُّهَا الۡكٰفِرُوۡنَ ۙ |
| I do not worship that which you worship, | LAA A,BUDU MA TA,BUDOON | لَاۤ اَعۡبُدُ مَا تَعۡبُدُوۡنَ ۙ |
| And you do not worship that which I worship. | WA LAA ANTUM AABIDUUNA MA A,BUD. | وَلَاۤ اَنۡتُمۡ عٰبِدُوۡنَ مَاۤ اَعۡبُدُ ۚ |
| And I shall not worship that Which you worship, | WA LAA ANAA AABIDUM-MAA ABAT-TUM. | وَلَاۤ اَنَا عَابِدٌ مَّا عَبَدۡتُّمۡ ۙ |
| And you will not worship that Which I worship. | WA LAA ANTUM AABIDUUNA MA A,BUD. | وَلَاۤ اَنۡتُمۡ عٰبِدُوۡنَ مَاۤ اَعۡبُدُ ؕ |
| You have your religion and I have my religion. | LA KUM DEENUKUM WALIYA DEEN. | لَكُمۡ دِيۡنُكُمۡ وَلِىَ دِيۡنِ ࣖ |

## THE ABUNDANCE (SURATUL KAWTHAR) سُوْرَةُ الْكَوْثَر

| | | |
|---|---|---|
| In the name of Allah the Most Kind, the Most Merciful. | BISMILLAAHIR-RAHMAANIR-RAHEEM. | بِسْمِ اللّٰهِ الرَّحْمٰنِ الرَّحِيْمِ |
| (O My prophet) surely we have given You the abundance. | INNAA A'TAINAAKAL-KAWTHAR. | اِنَّآ اَعْطَيْنٰكَ الْكَوْثَرَ ۝ط |
| So keep praying to your Lord And make sacrifice. | FASALLI LIRABBIKA WANHAR. | فَصَلِّ لِرَبِّكَ وَانْحَرْ ۝ط |
| Surely your enemy will be cut Off without name. | INNA SHAANI-AKA HUWAL ABTAR. | اِنَّ شَانِئَكَ هُوَ الْاَبْتَرُ ۝ع |

## THE BASIC NECESSITIES (SURATUL MAUUN) سُوْرَةُ الْمَاعُوْن

| | | |
|---|---|---|
| In the name of Allah the most Kind, the most Merciful. | BISMILLAAHIR-RAHMAANIR-RAHEEM. | بِسْمِ اللّٰهِ الرَّحْمٰنِ الرَّحِيْمِ |
| Have you seen him who denies the religion? | ARA'AYTALLADHI YUKADH-DHIBU BIDDEEN. | رَءَيْتَ الَّذِىْ يُكَذِّبُ بِالدِّيْنِ ۝ط |
| So he is the one who pushes away the orphan, | FADHAALIKAL-LADHI YADU'UL-YATEEM. | فَذٰلِكَ الَّذِىْ يَدُعُّ الْيَتِيْمَ ۝لا |
| and he does not urge others to Feed the needy. | WALAA YAHUDDU ALAA TA'AAMIL-MISKEEN. | وَلَا يَحُضُّ عَلٰى طَعَامِ الْمِسْكِيْنِ ۝ط |
| so woe is to those worshippers, | FA WAYLULLIL- MUSALLEEN. | فَوَيْلٌ لِّلْمُصَلِّيْنَ ۝لا |
| Who are careless of their Prayers, | ALLADHIINA HUM AN SALAATIHIM SAAHUUN. | الَّذِيْنَ هُمْ عَنْ صَلَاتِهِمْ سَاهُوْنَ ۝لا |
| Those who show off | ALLADHIINA HUM YURAA'UUN | الَّذِيْنَ هُمْ يُرَآءُوْنَ ۝لا |
| But refuse to give even the small help to others. | WA YAMNA-UUNAL-MAA'UUN. | وَيَمْنَعُوْنَ الْمَاعُوْنَ ۝ع |

## THE QURAYSH TRIBE (SURAH QURAYSH) سُوْرَةُ قُرَيْش

|  |  |  |
|---|---|---|
| In the name of Allah the Most kind, the Most Merciful. | BISMILLAAHIR-RAHMAANIR-RAHEEM. | بِسْمِ اللّٰهِ الرَّحْمٰنِ الرَّحِيْمِ |
| For Allah was to create love In the hearts of the Quraish, | LI IILAAFI QURAYSH. IILAAFIHIM | لِاِيْلٰفِ قُرَيْشٍ ۙ اٖلٰفِهِمْ |
| Love for their trade-journeys in Winter and summer. | RIHLATASH-SHITAA'I WASSAYF. | رِحْلَةَ الشِّتَآءِ وَالصَّيْفِ ۚ |
| So they should worship the Lord of this House | FALYA'BUDUU RABBA HAADHAL-BAYT. | فَلْيَعْبُدُوْا رَبَّ هٰذَا الْبَيْتِ ۙ |
| Who has provided them food Against hunger | ALLADHII AT'AMAHUM MIN JUU'IN' | الَّذِيْٓ اَطْعَمَهُمْ مِّنْ جُوْعٍ ۙ ۵ |
| And made them safe from fear. | WA AAMANAHUM-MIN KHAWF. | وَاٰمَنَهُمْ مِّنْ خَوْفٍ ۧ |

## THE ELEPHANT (SURAT-UL FEEL) سُوْرَةُ الْفِيْل

|  |  |  |
|---|---|---|
| In the name of Allah the Most Kind, the Most Merciful. | BISMILLAAHIR-RAHMAANIR-RAHEEM. | بِسْمِ اللّٰهِ الرَّحْمٰنِ الرَّحِيْمِ |
| (O prophet) Have you not seen How your Lord | ALAM TARA KAYFA FA'ALA | اَلَمْ تَرَ كَيْفَ فَعَلَ |
| Dealt with the people of the Elephant ? | RABBUKA BI-ASHAABIL-FEEL. | رَبُّكَ بِاَصْحٰبِ الْفِيْلِ ؕ |
| Did He not cause their schemes To end in failure? | ALAM YAJ'AL KAYDAHUM FI TADLEEL. | اَلَمْ يَجْعَلْ كَيْدَهُمْ فِيْ تَضْلِيْلٍ ۙ |
| And He sent against them The flocks of swallows, | WA ARSALA ALAYHIM TAYRAN ABAABEEL. | وَّاَرْسَلَ عَلَيْهِمْ طَيْرًا اَبَابِيْلَ ۙ |
| Which showered upon them the Hard pebbles of baked clay, | TARMIIHIM BIHIJARATIM-MIN SIJJEEL. | تَرْمِيْهِمْ بِحِجَارَةٍ مِّنْ سِجِّيْلٍ ۙ |
| So He made them like eaten Straw | FAJA'ALAHUM KA'ASFIM-MAKUUL. | فَجَعَلَهُمْ كَعَصْفٍ مَّاْكُوْلٍ ۧ |

# ISLAMIC MANNERS

|  |  |  |  |
|---|---|---|---|
| When doing something. | Say | بِسْمِ اللهِ | **BISMILLAH** *(In the name of Allah.)* |
| When meeting a muslim. | Say | اَلسَّلامُ عَلَيْكُم | **ASSALAMU ALAIKUM** *(Peace be upon you)* |
| When replying the salam. | Say | وَعَلَيْكُمُ السَّلام | **WA'ALAIKUMUS-SALAM** *(And peace be upon you)* |
| When getting up in the morning. | Say | لَآ اِلٰهَ اِلَّا الله | **LA ILAHA ILLALLAH** *(There is no god but Allah.)* |
| When sneezing. | Say | اَلْحَمْدُ لِله | **ALHAMDU LILLAH** *(Praise be to Allah)* |
| When hearing someone sneeze. | Say | يَرْحَمُكَ الله | **YARHAMU KALLAH** *(May Allah bless you)* |
| When hoping to do something. | Say | اِنْ شَآءَ الله | **INSHA ALLAH** *(If Allah wishes)* |
| To praise someone. | Say | سُبْحَانَ الله | **SUBHAN-ALLAH** *(Glory be to Allah)* |
| To appreciate someone. | Say | مَاشَآءَ الله | **MA SHA ALLAH** *(What Allah likes)* |
| To see someone off. | Say | فِيْ اَمَانِ الله | **FI AMAANILLAH** *(In the protection of Allah)* |
| To thank someone. | Say | جَزَاكَ الله | **JAZAKALLAH** *(May Allah give you reward.)* |
| To be sorry for a bad action. | Say | اَسْتَغْفِرُ الله | **ASTAGHFI-RULLAH** *(I ask Allah to forgive me)* |